CRUCIFIXION AND RESURRECTION:
A Pamphleteer Speaks

by

Apollo Starmule

Apollo Starmule

Apollo Polyhistor Starmule is one of the new breed of "soul geographers", an exponent of the new psychology which is millions of years young. This tract is a good, brief introduction to themes he treats in much greater detail in his astonishing novel of Speculative Mythology, *UNDO THE WINTER: The Odyssey of Sonny-Bob Culpepper*.

This Goode Booke Published By

SATYA YUGA BOOKS™
Asheville Weaverville Nacogdoches Tokyo

To the Daughter of Fire,
the Mother of Agni Yoga.

Let no doctrine stand in the way of
Attainment,
for no method can survive the onslaught of
Fire!

CRUCIFIXION AND RESURRECTION: A Pamphleteer Speaks

ISBN 978-0-9763230-1-3

Copyright © 2007 by Apollo Polyhistor Starmule

Cover Designed by Chris Master Using Exciting Fonts

Interior Designed by Apollo Starmule Using a More Dreary Font

"One should respect public opinion insofar as is necessary to avoid starvation and keep out of prison; anything that goes beyond this is voluntary submission to an unnecessary tyranny." --Bertrand Russell

"He knew his faults, or most of them. Knew the kind of sinning he liked and where to put his salt and he did not want to get acquainted with new likes and dislikes. As for sinning, most of the things he enjoyed were sins in the eyes of somebody. Except for reading . . . and most of his books were written by Pagan authors."
--From the novel *SITKA*
by Louis L'Amour

CHAPTER ONE: RAGNAROK!

It was more than winter's chill that brought the stranger to the little chapel in the hospital, more than a mere fear of going to hell . . . for hell had lately come to him, and was by turns blistering hot with the fires of Agni, and freezing cold with the energy of old terrors that the fires drove to the surface to be released.

The veil of the temple was tearing for him, the etheric web that surrounded his physical body was being ripped apart and burned away by nearly-physical, though unseen, fires directed at him by those who some would call Angels, though in the midst of his terror they appeared more as demons or as beasts of the forest to him.

Once a shadow-warrior charged with cleaning up the astral and etheric planes the human race had polluted with the selfishness of self-hatred for countless years, now he himself was being cleansed, though he did not know it. He believed himself under attack, and as the matter proceeded he danced around the little chapel trying to work up some energy to fight back, but all his ability at working with non-ordinary reality had fled, leaving him naked before the onslaught.

He had always been more interested in simply *doing*, as opposed to a more scholarly approach, and hadn't realized that the second half of his Fourth Initiation--the Crucifixion Initiation--would involve this terror. He had known he must fight and emerge victorious over his "Heimdall", as the guardian of the Rainbow Bridge was called by the Norse, and this he had done. And he had reflected after the fact that a cremation would have been appropriate, never realizing that was exactly what the Almighty had in store for him, and never realizing that since the Rainbow Bridge had permeated his entire being, that his entire being would have to be set aflame for years on end as he released the accumulated, refined karma of countless generations. But so it was.

And as he danced around this little hospital chapel, the only church he had been able to locate this winter's night whose doors were open, he was watched by the unblinking eye of the surveillance camera, an eye which he was aware of, but in his desperation he moved anyway, moved with the desperation of a man afire who was freezing to death with terror, a mad creature of fire and ice whose protective shield was entirely nonfunctional.

And soon the doors cast themselves open, and a woman involved in hospital administration appeared with a police officer, and to their questions he had the quickness of mind to reply that he prayed by doing performance art, and that that was his business on this dreary eve. This was enough--just barely--to save him from being arrested, but he was told by these generous Christians to quickly finish his prayers and leave the facility and not return. So with those he believed were demons all around him, and with the Christians behaving as though they themselves were influenced by demons, he sadly and with utmost terror finished his praying and left the chapel, and as he walked across the parking lot toward his little truck, he saw the hospital administrator walking toward a group of people who had gathered upon the asphalt, and he heard one of them offer a slight chiding to her, in a slightly unbelieving tone, for driving away a man who only wanted to pray.

In his dazed state, he started to move toward the woman to tell her goodbye, but then thought better of it and left the area as fast as he could.

And in retrospect, he wondered why there was no disciple to stand up for him, and to smite the ear off of the police officer with a sword. But then he shrugged, figuring it was for the best anyway, because he had never miraculously reattached an ear and didn't know how it was done, and such an action might have led to even greater troubles with the Romans of Haywood County, North Carolina.

Selah.

CHAPTER TWO: PISTOLS OR SWORDS?

I, even I, Apollo Polyhistor Starmule, was the stranger of the preceding chapter. And this little tract is my little testament to change.

I had had many non-ordinary experiences for years; indeed, my life was one long non-ordinary experience as I did the Sacred Work of refining the glamours and illusions out of human karma and releasing them to God to be transmuted or destroyed, as that Golden Force called God saw fit, thereby rendering the causal body--the soul body or Rainbow Bridge--of humanity itself a little cleaner, a little clearer, that it might come a little closer to reflecting the eternal Truth of Love, the truth that this Solar System was specifically formed to express.

My etheric body was shot to doll rags, full of holes and I was full of dismay long before the final battle with my own self-created Heimdall. That battle must occur so the Rainbow Bridge itself may be sacrificed that the full fusion of the personality with the Monad may be Achieved, with the soul serving as a sort of point of fusion that cements the Monad with the personality. Monad is to soul as soul is to personality, but with the full fusion of these three into one, the illusion of duality is forever destroyed and there is no more slavery to the glamours and illusions of matter.

Having been exhausted by my struggles for many earnest years, I had insufficient protection from my compromised etheric web and was tossed about on the currents of other people's emotions and "thought" processes to a degree that at times was almost unendurable. I didn't want access to their feelings and what passed for their thoughts, but I couldn't avoid it, with the result that many times I came near to a physical battle with one or another of the insensitive brutes. I just wanted to be left to Work my process in peace, untroubled by the currents they regarded as pleasure, but which I regarded as a dirty hell. For a person who is a slave to pleasure doesn't know true pleasure, he is simply an addict of distraction. He continually distracts himself so he may avoid feeling his own pain, but in his distraction lies much unneeded pain for any sensitive souls who come in contact with him. But dueling was illegal, so I couldn't do much to discipline these people.

I think when most people are consciously on the Path of Spiritual Achievement, that we will have to reinstate the civilized practice of dueling. People who are becoming conscious of their Selves don't fear death nearly so much as those who choose to remain unconscious, but they do fear the negative, unconscious, hate-filled waves these people continually unconsciously broadcast. Those waves are like a blow with a baseball bat to a sensitive person. It has always amazed me that if someone strikes you with a physical baseball bat you can legally defend yourself *and* the godless deviant criminal will also go to jail if you choose to report him and can prove the facts of the case. Yet an unconscious person, whether a news anchor or an unruly neighbor, can pollute the atmosphere of the neighborhood to such a degree that a sensitive person feels multiple blows from psychic baseball bats every day and can't legally defend herself. But this situation will change when a critical number of humans becomes conscious enough to take matters forcibly in hand and insist on introducing Beauty into the world to replace the ugliness that the governing entities have programmed the masses to worship.

CHAPTER THREE: Opium of the Masses

Well, I guess it's pretty obvious to anyone who has troubled themselves to look at the matter that the mass media has mostly taken over the role of religion as the opium of the masses.

Can it be doubted by anyone who is becoming civilized that most of the news anchors and reporters and media hosts of various kinds are little more than sophisticated animals, just beasts who continually allow themselves to be manipulated by nonhuman creatures who want to enslave Humanity? For they don't report on news, they report on the movements of an ancient astral cloud formed primarily of the energy of revenge. Thus do they help this old, tattered, ratty-assed cloud continue to work its own unconscious will upon human societies. They report the movements of this cloud as though these movements were real, but they are not real, they are formed of the glamour and illusion of revenge. And revenge is not real, does not exist, and cannot exist. For anyone who "avenges" himself on another person has in reality injured himself worse than he has injured the other person, though it may be a while before he can see this fact. So vengeance always remains undone, with each practitioner of this degraded "art" hurting himself worse than he ever hurts anyone else. It would be laughable, but somehow it has never caused me to laugh.

And so encouraging this illusion called revenge is the primary function of the mass media, and one of the primary functions of governments and of most religions. If you are an American, perhaps you remember the way the media treated Gulf War II in the early days; they treated it with the utmost fanfare, as though it were a glamorous football game, with the media cheering on its favorite team (the U.S. Military) with stirring, stimulating martial-sounding music. Where have we heard this before? Let me see . . . wasn't there something like this in the Thirties and Forties?

Now the media seems a little sheepish . . . I wonder why?

Let it be remembered that self-defense is a sacred right, and is one means of demonstrating the love we have for ourselves. But let this sacred right never be mistaken for the sour plum of vengeance that puckers the mouths with self-contempt of those who work in mass media.

It is beginning to appear less likely to me that the news media will ever be of any constructive use upon this planet, though occasionally we do see a movement toward forgiveness and redemption illustrated by the entertainment media. Yes, the entertainment media does mostly promote vengeance, but occasionally it does some good almost in spite of itself by promoting forgiveness, such as with the television sitcom *MY NAME IS EARL*. I'm no TV fan and hardly ever turn it on anymore, but I do occasionally make an effort to catch an episode of *MY NAME IS EARL*.   This program makes a largely-successful effort to illustrate the nature of karma and redemption without relying on that air-headed new-age nonsense that currently plagues the planet. There was a time when the term new-age was respectable, but that time is long past. Now it is time for real people to begin to redeem the planet, and for the new-agers to get out of the goddam way!

CHAPTER FOUR: Let Love Speak

Love is the eternal, splendid reality that "underlies the happenings of the times". It usually speaks to us with a gentle whisper unheeded by the mass media and governments and other religions of Cesar's conquest-minded depravity, but there are times when it speaks to the planet with a big fist of compassion. For suffering is the only method most of the blockheads in the world will respond to as a stimulating force toward experiencing, and then embodying, love.

If you want to understand the Mystery of Suffering, just look at how people deny love in their lives and that Mystery will stand perfectly revealed.

And most people are unaware that they've spent countless lives promoting the vengeance of suffering upon their neighbors, and thus upon themselves, so they may wonder why it takes so long to get clear. But it doesn't take so long to get clear; just a few lifetimes out of uncounted thousands or millions of lifetimes. Three or four incarnations is nothing compared to the time they've already spent behaving as damn fools.

Compassion is the full embodiment of love

thru *every* human faculty, so that no faculty is ever denied its proper expression, but learns to serve as a reflector of love into the world as that faculty expresses itself.

Really, Compassion is the full unification, the full coordination and synthesis, of Love with the joy of human Passion. At Liberation, we become a human embodiment of Compassion. Thus Liberated Human Beings are also known as the Lords of Compassion.

There was once a bumper sticker that said that cowboys make better lovers, but I think this would only be true if the particular cowboy in question was also a Lord of Compassion.

The Lords of Compassion, along with their slightly more advanced companions, the Masters of the Wisdom, bear little resemblance to the milksop image usually promoted by the new-agers. A Lord of Compassion can be a cowboy if he wants to, and a Master of the Wisdom can be a beautician or steelworker. And they can swill beer and eat meat, and their fornications have a delightfully light, sweet flavor. In other words, they are *human*. We never abandon our Humanity no matter how far we evolve; even if we evolve into a star or into a galaxy trillions of years from now, we will still carry our sweet, precious Humanity with us. For it is as Human Beings that we learn the lessons that we will apply daily when we become Divine Beings.

The only true spiritual mentor I ever had worked at a job that most of the fool new-agers would never have expected an Initiate of any degree to work at. Perhaps I was a bit of a fool new-ager at the time myself, for I asked him one day why he'd chosen the career he had. "The Light has to go to the darkness to shine," was his answer.

The Hierarchy of Light are not sexist. They use the terms "He", "His", and "Him" for both males and females simply because until recently there was too much prejudice in the world to dwell on the fact that there are female Masters of the Wisdom. In fact, it wouldn't surprise me if there are more female Lords of Compassion and Masters of the Wisdom than males, because females sometimes seem to learn the full expression of Compassion more quickly. In any case, the truth of the matter will soon be seen. Do not forget that the three disciples who brought the Light to the earth to kindle a new torch between 1870 and 1950 were all female. And they were all called *HE*.

CHAPTER FIVE: I'VE GOT YOUR MASTER

Those who make an effort to locate a Master will not find one. At best, if they are not too unlucky, they might find an Initiate of lower degree who has deluded himself that he is a Master. With such a one, they might be able to do some of the early stages of Work, though they would have karma with this Initiate to clear themselves from after they had learned what they could from kissing his hairy ass. And the most important lesson is that they never needed to kiss anyone's ass, and must learn to stand on their own two feet.

Those who go looking for a Master and have less pleasurable karma won't find even a true Initiate to take them in, but they will delude themselves into accepting a wicked sort of fake master known as the "Slayer of Souls". Oops.

True Masters don't advertise themselves and probably wouldn't admit to the title even if you were to meet one. They don't accept disciples who are so lazy they have to be told what to do; when to eat and what to eat, when to wipe their ass, etc. You'll run across some true Masters of the Wisdom, as well as

Initiates of still Higher Degree, if you simply go thru your ordinary life crafting your own fiery spiritual Path for yourself. But the objective cannot be to meet a Master, the objective must be World Service; perhaps more accurately, the objective must be World Creation or World Creativity. Because Creativity on every plane is how Love manifests itself. And must we say that true Creativity is not mere technical knowledge or ability?

I was once told by a rather famous martial arts grandmaster that it didn't matter which martial art I practiced. This gentleman is Liberated, and is known for saying that he "has no style", despite the fact that he does teach a specific style. But he has transcended the limitations of martial arts systems to arrive at a full expression of Creativity.

Yet practically all of this gentleman's higher-ranking students would say that it does matter which style of martial art you practice, and that it has to be their art! Well, we see the difference between a Liberated person and a mere technician, don't we?

Early in the twentieth century, many martial arts died out because the Master of the Art could find no student worthy to pass the title on to. Does such worthiness come of technical ability? No, it does not. It does not even come of an ability to sensitize yourself and work with energy. Rather, there is a secret that must be experienced, and most martial arts practitioners have no idea that this secret even exists. Those who know it have never told it, and have no need to speak of it among themselves. You won't find it written down anywhere. Yet the "secret" is so obvious it is no secret at all. It is so much in the open that nobody can see it.

Don't be glamoured by the term "Master". A martial arts "Master" is seldom a Master of the Wisdom; a "Zen Master" is seldom a Master of the Wisdom. And those few who actually have attained this degree of Illumination put their pants on the same way you do, they are just more aware of the process of getting dressed.

CHAPTER SIX: THE FEMININE INFLUENCE

The feminine influence is indispensable in attaining to Illumination. Sophia, the Holy Ghost, is of course the feminine influence involved in simply knowing, and in translating that knowingness into some form that others can relate to on some level.

The Bible says that the "sin against the Holy Ghost" is the only sin that cannot be forgiven. Well, this is archaic language and may have been slightly mistranslated, anyway.

But the Bible does speak rightly on this point. What the Bible actually means, translated into modern lingo, is that when someone derides or speaks against the words of an Illumined Human Being, that person has spoken against the Holy Ghost, the Sophia, that animates the thoughts and visionings of that Illuminated Human Being. And this is such a severe crime that the sinner won't be able to recover from his sin in his present life, but will only be able to recover in a future incarnation. Since God is Love, he will be presented with the opportunity for that future incarnation.

The "sin against the Holy Ghost" has nothing to do with agreement or disagreement; nobody is obligated to agree with anything anyone else says, even if the speaker is a Master of the Wisdom, or even if the speaker is Senior even to the Masters of the Wisdom. And disagreement is a silly waste of time. No, the "sin against the Holy Ghost" is simply trying to deny the right of a Sophia-Illumined human being his own Voice. Or trying to deny yourself your own Voice, if you have felt the touch of Sophia and then returned to the hog-trough of a materialist approach to religion or science or any other aspect of Life.

Fundamentalism in any form is the "sin against the Holy Ghost". To work one's way free of fundamentalism is to find oneself embraced by the feminine influence. Yet if one is a "feminist" in the sense of some of the modern females, they have missed contact with their own origin because they are fundamentalists. Political correctness is the liberal form of fundamentalism.

The only thing you can do with a person who has committed the "sin against the Holy Ghost" is to shake the dust off your shoes and walk away from them and never look back.

Nobody is perfect; the Masters can make mistakes too, though their mistakes are of a higher order because they are not born of lust, of material delusion. So no one can speak with the voice of authority for any other person. Each person must find their own Voice, their own position of relationship within Sophia's embrace. The genuine Masters will not try to override your Voice with their own, for they know that Sophia does not conflict with Sophia, though she does taste differently depending upon the unique individual nature of the person whose lungs she is breathing into in any particular moment. Being embraced by Sophia is like being embraced by a Goddess, which is appropriate for me, because the Goddess ignites my Passion, and my Compassion, on all levels.

I taste like a hamburger, I guess, but in Sophia's embrace I become the best of burgers and am quite nourishing in my fullbodied way. My friend has a lighter taste, I would say something like an Illumined squash or some similar vegetable.

CHAPTER SEVEN: THE ASHRAMS

An Ashram is a group of conscious souls
working with souls who are making progress
at becoming conscious. The Work is, of
course, simply forming a chalice to catch the
Love of the Solar System and exhibit it
Creatively in every dimension which the
Ashram touches. Heinlein's Church of All
Worlds in his bestselling novel *STRANGER IN
A STRANGE LAND* could be considered an
Ashram.

The Ashrams exist in the Subtle
Dimensions. They have not been physically
present for a very long time. Eventually--
and perhaps sooner rather than later--they
will begin to "condense" themselves back
into physical manifestation. Woo Woo.

Sometimes folk from one Ashram have
trouble understanding folk from another
Ashram. Sometimes Masters of the Wisdom
even have trouble understanding folk from
an Ashram other than their own. We are
told that at a certain level of Illumination
beyond that which the Masters and Chohans
have attained that such problems will vanish.
I guess it will take a while for this theory to
be tested.

There are seven major Ashrams, each one

of which contains seven subsidiary Ashrams. So there are forty-nine subsidiary Ashrams within the overlighting embrace of the seven major Ashrams. We have just performed a feat of multiplication. So primary school math instruction wasn't totally wasted on us.

You experience a different flavor from one Ashram to the next. The lovefest that is an Ashram will play out in a more-or-less different manner from one Ashram to another. So Truth, which is itself the child of Love, comes in many flavors to suit every palate. The difficulty is when beginners rigidify themselves by imagining their flavor is the only one that has an authentic taste. When they make this mistake, it isn't long before they lose even the taste of their own Ashram.

Sometimes people imagine a conflict between two or more spiritual teachings which doesn't exist. They think teaching A contradicts teaching B. Nah, that don't never happen, not really. If they are authentic, they will not contradict each other, it's just that a specialist in interpreting teaching A may not have much ability at interpreting teaching B, even though the essence of the two teachings is practically identical. The outer form and flavor provide a unique path which the disciple trods to arrive at the essence, and since it is so hard to walk even one path, it is no wonder that folk have trouble reconciling two paths. But the eternal destination is the same, regardless of which path emanating from which Ashram is chosen.

Someday, all human beings will be Liberated Human Beings, and at that time a full coordination will be Achieved between the human kingdom and the Spiritual Kingdom, because the human kingdom will have itself become the Spiritual Kingdom. This will have occurred because human beings on a massive scale will have chosen to Work to spiritualize their consciousness. There will come a point at which those who have not chosen to do this Work can no longer incarnate on this earth. They will be "held over" until a new class forms, millions of years after those humans who chose to Work have been Liberated.

And there is no Liberation for Self. Only Self as a part of Whole can know Liberation. There is no consciousness of separation or duality in Liberation.

Know the movement of Whole and you know the movement of Self. Know the movement of Self only, and you know only illusion.

CHAPTER EIGHT: IMAGINING A WORLD THAT ISN'T STUPID

Stupidity is sourced in laziness, which itself is the child of fear. So stupidity vanishes as we learn to release fear. And no lazy person can learn to release fear, because releasing old energies is very hard work.

Stupidity is not Destiny. No person is destined to be stupid. So when a person chooses to behave stupidly, they are running away from their own sweet Destiny, their own tallest standing in the Cosmos of Love.

The mass media is founded upon stupidity and run by the stupid. They run from their own Destiny in order to manipulate you into remaining fearful so that you will be as stupid as they are. They think their egotisms are safe if they can keep the public stupid. Of course, these observations must also be applied to governments, and to most religions.

So when the public finally learns to Work to release fear, then its laziness, its spiritual torpor, will begin to vanish and therefore its stupidity will begin to vanish. A great glow of Lovingkindness will overspread the earth, embracing every one who is willing to Work like the wings of a rosy Angel. And everyone who Works will feel safe in the arms of this rosy Angel, and thus will be unaffected by the mass media and the other branches of government.

Soon all these governing agencies will vanish in an activity of Lovingkindness of which there has never been an equal in the millions upon millions of years of earth-human history. Destiny will be seen as a *right* earned thru Work and no one will ever try to deny you your Destiny again.

But you have to be willing to call a spade a spade, honey. First you have to tell those who would interfere with your approach to your Destiny to go to hell, then walk that Path to your Destiny with head held high in self-esteem and self-compassion. Egotism must be abandoned before true self-esteem and self-compassion can manifest. Egotism is a rigid trap, but your Destiny waits as a rosy glow upon your horizon that can only be approached thru a compassionate flexibility.

Watch the talking heads in the media, whether "news" or "entertainment", manipulate public opinion to condemn and find guilty those who go on trial, when the defendant has some quirk that makes him an easy target or unpopular with large segments of the public. The media always plays to the lowest common denominator and slanders almost without appearing to do so because the sense of entitlement it has programmed the public to give to it will let it get away with murder, half the time. Yet these soul-poor media people have no idea what they do to themselves with the jokes they play upon others.

Destiny, then, is a child of self-love, self-esteem, self-compassion. It plays to the highest common denominator, which is the human soul (the home of all true intelligence), so when we play for Destiny, we will suddenly find we live in a society which is no longer stupid.

CHAPTER NINE: SEX, THE ORIGINAL RELIGION

It is ironic that the original form of human worship should be considered a sin by the so-called "major" religions! Hell, they aren't even major religions in any true sense, because they leave the original religion out of their festivities, if their death-oriented practices can be considered festivities. The original religion is the foundation of all true religions. The original religion is sex.

The human race in its early days, millions upon millions of years ago, was androgynous. You couldn't tell the chicks from the guys, because all were both chicks and guys. They didn't have sex, and they didn't have worship. They did have some consciousness of the divine that was built into them, but it was sort of automatic, almost on the level of instinct. They didn't understand the value of connection because they had no way to physically illustrate the value of connection to themselves. So they had no worship, because worship *is* connection. Worship is connection to other worshippers, and it is connection to God, and it is connection to the gods and goddesses that God made as representatives and custodians of God's thoughts. Every god or goddess is a thought in the mind of God, representing some force that the mind of God has devised for some constructive purpose.

Yo, anyhow, the day came when, under an impulse from the Mind of God, the representatives and custodians of God's thoughts took it upon themselves to encourage the separation into two sexes of the human race. Then they introduced humans to sex, and used sex to introduce humans to worship . . . to connection! And ever since sex has been the basis of connection and of creativity upon this globe.

Those who would enslave humanity have used their propaganda apparatus (mass media and other sources) to degrade sex (worship, connection) in the minds of the public, so that now sex is seen as something you *get*, rather than as a gift you share. The result is that there is little connection in the world, because everyone is trying to rob everyone else of what originally was a gift that everyone had in common. Little connection means that little true worship occurs, so that with the degradation of sex, all worship has been degraded into a mere leisure activity, instead of being approached in a sacred spirit of connectedness. Yes, worship can be fun, but when the element of sacredness is removed, the fun becomes a mere shell of itself and becomes more of a distraction or addiction than true fun. True fun is not addictive, nor does it distract you from the meaning of life. True fun meshes with the meaning of life to provide you with a wholebody experience of compassionate sacredness. True fun can be a component of the meaning of life.

Beauty is the meaning of life. The fact that we are beautiful in one another's arms is the direct illustration of the meaning of life. The experience of true Beauty is a prayer of togetherness. Therefore, let us learn to pray again thru the sacred medium of sex.

CHAPTER TEN: WHEN IS LUCRE NOT
FILTHY?

I read somewhere that baby shit was sacred.
If I remember correctly, the point the author
was trying to make is that everything is
sacred, so money must be sacred too. It is
therefore okay to make and enjoy money.

Well, I've got news for that author: baby
shit is *not* sacred, and neither is any other
kind of shit. Shit only becomes sacred once
nature's processes have turned it back into
soil. Transformation or transmutation are
necessary before any sort of waste becomes
sacred. Soil is sacred; the shit that grew by
natures processes into soil is not sacred. But
this is what we discerning types have to deal
with all the time: immature people who
don't know how to practice discernment and
who thus mislead themselves and those who
depend on their observations.

Let it be said that it is a false analogy to
compare baby shit to money. Baby shit is
waste, and waste is a stagnant form of
energy that awaits rebirth in a new form thru
the recycling process of nature. Money is an
active, powerful form of energy, so long as
the motive one brings to it is a worthy one.
In other words, as long as you are using

money to serve a cause greater than yourself, money can be useful. It only becomes filthy lucre when used to serve yourself.

This doesn't mean that you can't use money to take care of yourself; of course you can. As you serve that cause that is greater than yourself, you know yourself as a part of that cause, and you are automatically taken care of and provided with what you need to manifest your lifestream fully upon the physical earth in whatever way is appropriate to you and your own mission to contact and then embody your Destiny. Using money in this way renders money holy, or at least turns it into a tool, an accoutrement, that can be used to serve the holy.

For example, suppose you have a Vision of a genuinely loving, compassionate family and you want to bring this healthful Vision into outward manifestation on the earth. You will use your money to serve your family. You won't serve them with luxury, because luxury represents decay and a stagnating death, but you will serve them with quality, because quality is a characteristic of spirituality, a characteristic of soul. If you buy a chair from the more-or-less spiritually aware craftsman down the street, you will have bought a product that the craftsman infused with a bit of his own spirit, a bit of his own spiritual quality. So spending your money in service to a quality experience for your family is a good thing, because it gifts them with a better quality of energy-experience. Spending your money on mass produced merchandise may sometimes be acceptable, depending on circumstances, but is to be avoided anytime something better is available. However, it pays to remember that just because an item is hand-produced, it doesn't necessarily radiate quality; it may radiate the egotism of someone who wants to do something better than his neighbors, and just because an item is mass-produced, it doesn't necessarily mean that it is worthless, or even inferior. You must develop your own discernment to sense the energy that is appropriate to gift your family with in each moment, and then your use of money will almost always be an evolutionary Achievement.

"Live long and prosper!"

CHAPTER ELEVEN: DEVAS AND NATURE SPIRITS

Well, there's nothing we can do about it. Devas and nature spirits are everywhere so we might as well get used to the fact and learn to work with the little beggars.

Deva is another word for Angel; nature spirits will one day evolve into devas, just as human beings are evolving themselves toward the objective of becoming Lords of Compassion. From nature spirit to deva; from human being to Lord of Compassion. Evolution into lovingkindness is the eternal way of nature.

But the little farts get on my nerves. They are everywhere, and you can't go anywhere without stumbling all over them. They are here right now even as I type these lines . . . and of course, even I welcome some of their activities, because inspirational devas hover around me as author, giving me impulses that translate into words on the page. I am receptive to inspiration.

But when the fuckers are tugging on your pants leg or pretending to be a cat scratching your leg, I get somewhat aggravated. I used to get more than aggravated; I used to get scared shitless.

But a human being can get used to any sort of situation if it continues long enough . . . and they have done some good work with me in terms of helping me become healthy and, believe it or not, far less stressed out. In the beginning they added enormously to my stress, but now they've burned most of the stress away thru their crazy, unusual means and I'm better than I ever was before.

I think in some ways I'm even prettier than I was before, though I'm not dogmatic in this claim. Certainly, while my energy bodies have been totally reconstructed, my physical body has also registered many changes. My chiropractor has sort of kept track of some of the physical changes, though I don't think she is fully aware of all of them. I still wish my penis were bigger, but I guess it takes time to build a larger penis. I guess I'm pretty satisfied with my testicles and scrotum. And really, my penis is pretty large as long as it is erect. But it sort of curls up and looks a little sullen when flaccid.

But it seems conceivable to me that you didn't buy this sacred tract to hear about my penis. If you did, perhaps you know someone who can refer you to a good therapist.

Do you know that relatively famous little statue of Freyr, the Norse fertility god? He's holding his penis up to his nose. How about that?

Just goes to show you that some cultures wouldn't flip out over seeing a nipple on primetime television.

Some cultures actually admit to having religious organs, sexual organs. I guess maybe we could call them religio-sexual organs, bodily contrivances made for sharing in the holy bliss of person-to-person communion, while the gods and goddesses of our pantheon look on, encouraging us with merry smiles, laughing eyes, and with the occasional penis held to their nose.

CHAPTER TWELVE: A SENSE OF HUMOR

Politically correct people and other forms of fundamentalists can't become Liberated because their sense of humor is underdeveloped. You have to both be an optimist and have a sense of humor to be able to have a snowball's chance in hell of Achieving Liberation. The ancient Norse knew this, which is why their gods were often so jolly and got even jollier each evening when they got drunk.

You can tell that politicians have no chance at even understanding that Liberation is possible, let alone Achieving it. When was the last time you heard a politician make a joke about the last time he broke the law? Yet many of these politicians have broken the law, whether by pursuing sexual favors from subordinates or driving down the road drunk and/or on drugs. Yet politicians are the very people who scream loudest for the drug war, and who sponsor that war, and who sponsor all kinds of laws supposedly aimed at forcing puritanical standards on other people's sexuality. When Mark Twain called Congress "America's only permanent criminal class," he wasn't joking. They are criminally insane.

Evolutionaries only survive by having a sense of humor. Yes, they'll probably get outraged from time to time and go on the warpath to right some injustice, but their sense of humor is one of their most important survival mechanisms. Evolutionaries can't be politicians! A good joke is always politically incorrect.

But let us avoid the motive of trying to bring distress to another as we joke our way thru this strange life. People who deliberately use jokes to wound, even in slight degree, have one or more of their chakras spinning backwards and exhibit self-hate thru their jokes. Yet those who take offense at a good joke simply because it is politically incorrect hurt themselves, and are not to be catered to by the sensitive evolutionary.

Sometimes we may joke, or make some other type of statement, from a feeling of frustration. The idiots may mistake the frustration for malice, but it is not. And it is hard not to get frustrated with the foot-dragging idiots who occupy nearly all the positions of authority in almost every sort of arena. They are not evolutionaries, though some of them are new-agers. But a fundamentalist new-ager is doing nothing to bring about the merging of heaven and earth, and is just pissing in the wine at the wedding. I consider this to be rude.

It is a pitiful thing to be ruled by a theology. No book is fit to rule over a human being, and no book *can* rule over a human being who is becoming aware. Use books wisely, and treat the good ones as friends, but know that their primary purpose is to quicken you energetically and stimulate your imagination, and maybe to make you laugh or give you a grin from time to time as you imagine the author playing with his penis or performing somesuch trick.

What is Wisdom? Wisdom is simply Love-In-Action. So it is obvious that Wisdom is fresh in each moment; hence the term Ageless Wisdom. Is it not evident that Wisdom is not a collection of knowledgings or a system of breathing exercises or a sitting upon the ass in meditation?

Don't treat the words of the Masters of the Wisdom as dogma; they don't want slaves, they want co-servers who can find their own way into Paradise.

NOTES

You may use this space to write your own feelings
as you are stirred into a new Livingness
by a freshly quickened imagination

www.ingramcontent.com/pod-product-compliance
Lightning Source LLC
Chambersburg PA
CBHW061757040426
42447CB00011B/2339